IT'S COOL TO LEARN ABOUT COUNTRIES

Social Studies Explorer

CHINA

➤ by Lucia Raatma

CHERRY LAKE PUBLISHING • ANN ARBOR, MICHIGAN

Published in the United States of America
by Cherry Lake Publishing
Ann Arbor, Michigan
www.cherrylakepublishing.com

Content Adviser: Huaiyin Li, PhD, Associate Professor,
Department of History, University of Texas at Austin

Book design: The Design Lab

Photo credits: Cover, ©iStockphoto.com/PictureLake; cover and page 1, ©iStockphoto.
com/joebrandt; page 4, ©iStockphoto.com/hippostudio; page 5, ©iStockphoto.com/xxz114;
page 7, ©iStockphoto.com/pfrank1978; page 8, ©iStockphoto.com/Halstenbach; page
10, ©iStockphoto.com/gioadventures; page 12, ©iStockphoto.com/PhotoTalk; page 13,
©iStockphoto.com/samkee; page 14, ©iStockphoto.com/bo1982; page 16, ©Copestello/
Dreamstime.com; page 18, ©iStockphoto.com/LDF; page 19, ©iStockphoto.com/Nikada; page
20, ©vario images GmbH & Co.KG/Alamy; page 22, ©iStockphoto.com/travelphotographer;
page 25, ©iStockphoto.com/monkeybusinessimages; page 26, ©iStockphoto.com/mrloz; page
27, ©iStockphoto.com/yenwen; page 28 top, ©Lieska/Dreamstime.com; page 28 bottom,
©iStockphoto.com/JulienGrondin; page 30, ©Shiningcolors/Dreamstime.com; page 31,
©iStockphoto.com/beemore; page 32, ©Eastimages/Dreamstime.com; page 33, ©iStockphoto.
com/araraadt; page 36, ©Vclements/Dreamstime.com; page 37, ©Ongchangwei/Dreamstime.
com; page 39, ©iStockphoto.com/azmiman; page 40, ©iStockphoto.com/YinYang; pages 41
and 45, ©iStockphoto.com/izusek; page 42, ©iStockphoto.com/TonnyWong

Library of Congress Cataloging-in-Publication Data
Raatma, Lucia.
    It's cool to learn about countries—China / by Lucia Raatma.
        p. cm.—(Social studies explorer)
    Includes bibliographical references and index.
    ISBN-13: 978-1-60279-823-6
    ISBN-10: 1-60279-823-0
    1. China—Juvenile literature. I. Title. II. Series.
    DS706.R28 2010
    951—dc22   2010000475

Cherry Lake Publishing would like to acknowledge the work of The Partnership for 21st
Century Skills. Please visit *www.21stcenturyskills.org* for more information.

Printed in the United States of America
Corporate Graphics Inc.
July 2010
CLFA07

TABLE OF CONTENTS

CHAPTER ONE

WELCOME TO CHINA!

A traditional Chinese boat, known as a junk, sails across Victoria Harbour, Hong Kong.

Would you like to visit China? It is the world's fourth-largest country. It also has the world's largest population, with more than 1.3 billion people. The country's official name is People's Republic of China. China is home to many different cultures. The land is beautiful.

Its people are proud of their incredible works of art and delicious food.

Are you ready to take a trip through China, culture explorer? Where could you start? You could travel the Yangtze River. Or you could explore the Great Wall of China. You could visit the National Art Museum in Beijing. You might also take in the sights of a parade during Chinese New Year. Depending on the time of year and where you go, you might wear shorts. Or you might be more comfortable in a heavy jacket. Let's explore China!

The history of the Great Wall of China dates back thousands of years. But most of the wall that has survived dates back to the late 15th century. The wall was built to protect China from attack. The entire structure is estimated to be 5,500 miles (8,851 kilometers) long.

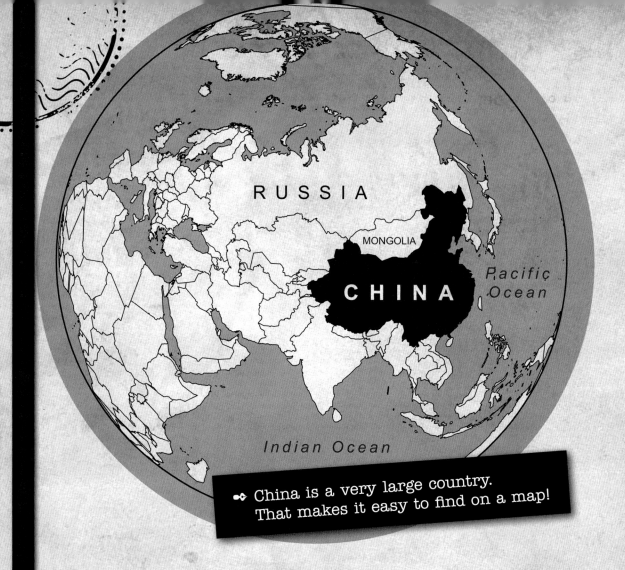

RUSSIA

MONGOLIA

CHINA

Pacific Ocean

Indian Ocean

China is a very large country.
That makes it easy to find on a map!

Where in the world is China? It is located on the continent of Asia. Look at a globe. You'll find China just below Russia and Mongolia.

China extends for 3,705,407 square miles (9,596,961 square kilometers). One way to think of China is to divide it into different areas: the Eastern Zone, the Northwestern Zone, and the Southwestern Zone. Each of these regions has different animals, plants, and weather.

The Eastern Zone is known for its rich farmland. Parts of the Yellow (or Huang He) River and Yangtze River flow through the region. They help bring water to the fields and rice crops. The Yangtze is the third-longest river in the world. It stretches 3,960 miles (6,373 km) across China. The upper part of the Eastern Zone was once called Manchuria. It has meadows, forests, and huge plains for farming.

The Yangtze River is one of the most distinctive landmarks in China.

➥ The Gobi Desert is estimated to have an area of about 500,000 square miles (1, 294, 994 square kilometers).

The Northwestern Zone contains the Gobi Desert. The Gobi stretches from northern China into Mongolia. It is one of the world's largest deserts. The Taklimakan Desert is also in this region. Some areas are so dry that no animals or plants can live there. The Turfan Depression is home to Lake Aiding. This is a salt lake that is 505 feet (154 meters) below sea level. This is the lowest point in China.

The Southwestern Zone features mountains, canyons, and **plateaus**. Its most famous mountain range is the Himalaya. These mountains are located in Tibet. Many people think that Tibet should be its own country. But the Chinese government claims it as part of China. Mount Everest, in the Himalaya, is the highest mountain peak on Earth. It is 29,035 feet (8,850 m) tall.

yeti

What's a yeti? It is the name given to a creature that some people believe lives in the Himalaya. You may know it as the abominable snowman. Scientists have not been able to find evidence that yetis exist.

➼ Beijing is the center of government activity in China.

The capital of China is Beijing. But the city of Shanghai has a larger population. Other large cities include Tianjin, Guangzhou, and Chongqing. Hong Kong and Macau are two territories that belong to China. They are located to the southeast of the **mainland**. Taiwan is an island to the east of China. It is known as the Republic of China.

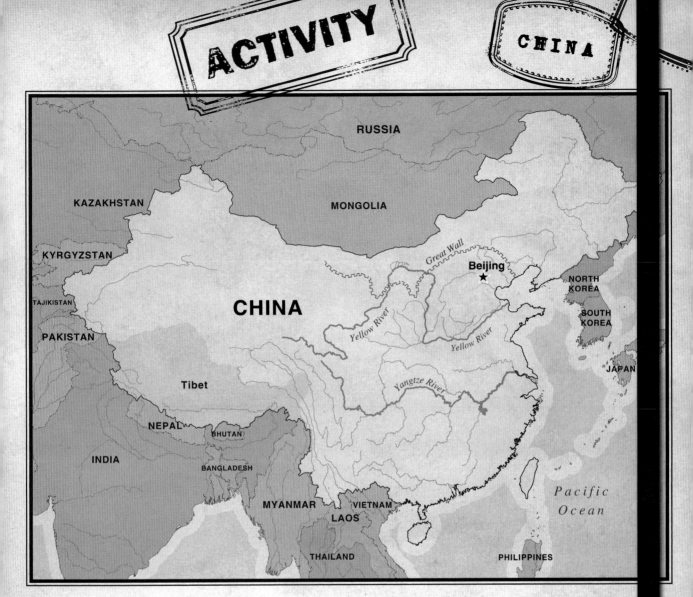

Practice your skills as a mapmaker. Look at the map of China above. Place a piece of paper over the map and trace the outline of the country. See where Beijing is? Mark that city with a star on your tracing. Also label the Great Wall and Tibet. Now, label the Yangtze River and the Yellow River. Do you see how the Yangtze River cuts through the center of China? As you work, pay attention to which countries border China.

❖ Snow is a common part of winter weather in some parts of the country.

China is so big that its weather varies greatly from place to place. In the Eastern Zone, there are hot summers and cold winters. The Northwestern Zone can experience hot weather, with temperatures at times nearing 100 degrees Fahrenheit (38 degrees Celsius) in desert areas. Much of the rest of northwestern China, however, experiences very chilly winters. The Southwestern Zone can be very cold along the western border and milder toward the center of the country.

Monsoons are heavy winds that often bring rainstorms during the summer. Most of China receives rain

during the monsoon season. The season lasts from May until October each year. The country can also be hit with typhoons. These storms are similar to hurricanes and form in the Pacific Ocean.

If you visit China, you may be amazed at the number of different plants and animals. In fact, China has more than 30,000 types of plants and trees! Bamboo is one interesting plant. This is a woody grass that can grow very tall. China also has more than 1,000 types of birds and hundreds of reptiles. Some of China's animals are **endangered**. These include the Asiatic elephant and the giant panda.

Giant pandas live deep in the mountains of China. China is their only native country. But pandas have been given to zoos throughout the world. These endangered animals feed on bamboo. Fewer than 2,500 giant pandas still live in the wild.

bamboo

BUSINESS AND GOVERNMENT IN CHINA

↬ The people of China work hard at many different kinds of jobs.

The Chinese civilization is one of the oldest in the world. It dates back thousands of years. As the nation has grown and changed, its people have remained committed to hard work. Duty and responsibility are important values.

There are many businesses that keep China's economy strong. These companies have an important international **export** industry. Did you know that there's a good chance you use Chinese products every day? Think about your TV. It probably came from an electronics store. It's likely that the store bought its TVs from China. What other industries are important in China?

IMPORT EXPORT

Do you want to know more about China's economy? One important piece of information is its trading partners. Trading partners are the countries that **import** goods from a country or export goods to that country. Here is a graph showing China's top import and export partners.

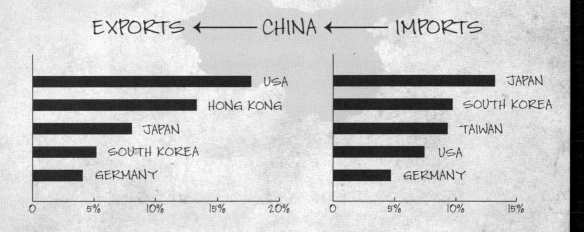

EXPORTS ← CHINA ← IMPORTS

EXPORTS	IMPORTS
USA	JAPAN
HONG KONG	SOUTH KOREA
JAPAN	TAIWAN
SOUTH KOREA	USA
GERMANY	GERMANY

Chinese money is called renminbi. This word means "people's currency." Individual units of money include yuan coins and bills. There are also jiao coins and fen coins. In 2010, one U.S. dollar equaled approximately 6.8 yuan.

Farming is an important business in China. Chinese farmers grow rice, wheat, potatoes, and peanuts. Other crops include tea, barley, and cotton. Farmers also raise chickens, pigs, cattle, goats, and sheep. Less than 20 percent of China's land is good for farming. Still, nearly half of the country's people work in agriculture. Many people make a living by fishing in China's lakes and rivers. They catch more carp than any other kind of fish.

According to the CIA World Factbook (www.cia.gov/library/publications/the-world-factbook/), approximately 40 percent of Chinese people work in agriculture. Manufacturing makes up 27 percent of the nation's labor force. Service industries made up 33 percent.

Using this information, create a bar graph that shows these parts of China's economy. Ask a teacher or other adult for help if you need it. Label the horizontal axis of the bar graph "Type of Industry." Label the vertical axis "Percentage of Chinese Workers." Don't forget to label each bar with the correct industry. Which bar will be the longest? Which will be the shortest?

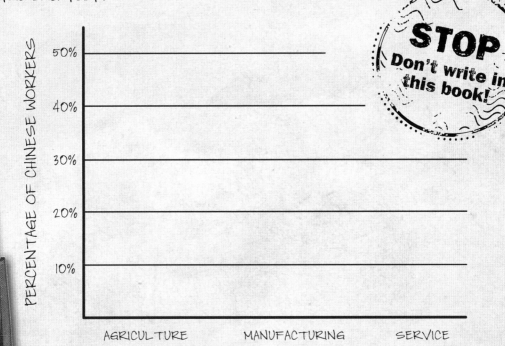

China's factories produce many items. These include cement, steel, and machinery. Factories export electronics, clothing, toys, and sporting goods. Factory life is not easy. Workers do not make a lot of money. Sometimes the workplaces are not safe.

Have you ever used a compass during a hike? You probably were happy to know what direction you were heading in. The compass is just one of many inventions that come from China. Other important items from China include kites and toothbrushes.

China relies on service workers to keep the country running. Service workers provide a service instead of a product. Such workers include teachers, doctors, and government officials.

The government of China is led by a **communist** party. Communism is a certain system of government. One idea behind communism is that property should belong to the entire country instead of specific people. The Chinese government, however, began to change its system in the late 1970s. For example, it has opened its economy to private business and ownership.

The city of Shanghai is one of China's major economic centers.

The governing body of China is the National People's Congress (NPC). Its members come from different regions of the country. The president and vice president of China are elected by the NPC for 5-year terms. The premier is nominated by the president and confirmed by the NPC. The premier is the head of government.

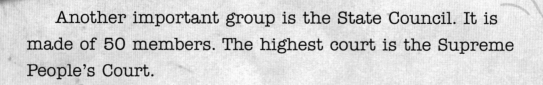

Hu Jintao became president of China in March 2003. Xi Jinping became vice president in March 2008. Wen Jiabao became premier in 2003.

Hu Jintao

Another important group is the State Council. It is made of 50 members. The highest court is the Supreme People's Court.

◆ The Chinese flag was adopted in 1949. It is red, with one large yellow star and four smaller stars.

Governing a country as large and diverse as China is difficult. There are 23 **provinces** in China. Each has its own local government. The four big cities—Beijing, Shanghai, Tianjin, and Chongqing—report directly to the central government. Hong Kong and Macau have a special status. In addition, there are five regions that are **autonomous**. They are treated differently, and are made up primarily of **minority** groups. Let's learn more about these groups and meet the people of China.

CHAPTER THREE

MEET THE PEOPLE

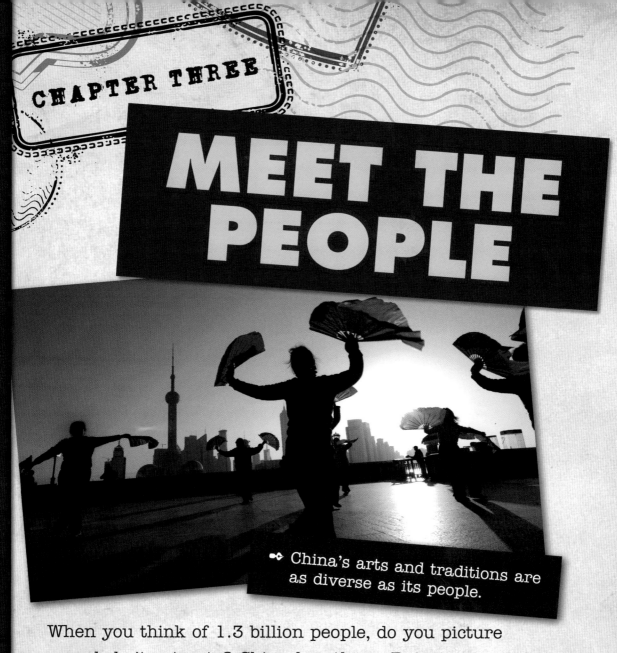

➻ China's arts and traditions are as diverse as its people.

When you think of 1.3 billion people, do you picture crowded city streets? China has those. But many people also live in the country. In fact, 57 percent of Chinese people live in **rural** areas. The remaining 43 percent live in **urban** areas.

There are 56 different **ethnic** groups in China. The largest is the Han. This group represents more than 90

percent of China's people. The other 55 cultural groups are minority groups. They include the Tibetan, Mongol, Manchu, and many others. Even though they are minorities, they total approximately 91 million people.

The official language of China is Mandarin Chinese. More than 50 percent of the people can speak it. This language is also called Putonghua. Many minority groups speak their own languages. Cantonese is often spoken in southern China. Some groups also speak different versions of Mandarin.

CHINESE

Let's learn some Mandarin Chinese words and phrases. Look at the list below. On a separate sheet of paper, try to match the Mandarin words with the English translations. See the answers below.

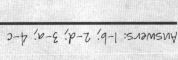

STOP
Don't write in this book!

MANDARIN	ENGLISH
1. qing (cheeng)	a. hello
2. xie xie (she-eh she-eh)	b. please
3. ni hao (nee how)	c. good-bye
4. zai-jian (zigh-jee-in)	d. thank you

When you see Chinese words, they may be written using characters from the alphabet you already know. The written Chinese language, however, traditionally uses pictographs. These are characters that express ideas or individual words. There are more than 3,000 pictographs in the Chinese language.

Chinese pictographs are very beautiful. Here is one that can mean home or family, depending on how it is used:

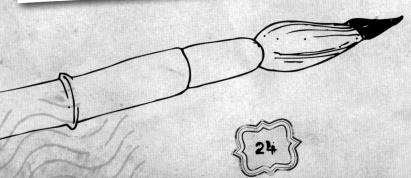

❧ Family life is important no matter where you go in China.

Family life in China can vary from place to place. In some areas, a family may share the home with grand-parents, aunts, and uncles. For many years—as in many parts of the world—men were thought of as masters of the home. Women were expected to obey them. This is slowly changing. Women increasingly hold jobs outside the home, working in industries such as business, law, and education.

Chinese children are expected to get at least a 9-year education. Students study many different subjects, including math, language, and history. Students may also study English. Approximately 90 percent of Chinese people know how to read.

China has more than 1,500 colleges and universities. To be admitted, students have to pass a national test. Competition to get into the best schools is fierce.

•❖ Some Chinese students study science and technology in college.

❧ China is known for the beautiful art of calligraphy.

Chinese people have a strong appreciation for art. Calligraphy, poetry, and painting are known as the Three Perfections in China. Calligraphy is a system and art of beautiful handwriting. Sometimes the three art forms are combined into single works of art. China is also known for beautiful statues. Many fine pieces of art are made from jade and porcelain, too. Jade is a type of hard, green stone. Porcelain is a type of fine pottery used to make different objects.

Confucius

Confucius was a Chinese thinker and philosopher who lived from 551 BCE. to 479 BCE. Many of his ideas have influenced groups through the centuries. One of his famous quotations is translated as, "What you do not wish for yourself, do not do to others."

Buddha →

The Chinese people practice a wide variety of religions. The largest group is Buddhist. They follow the teachings of a religious leader named Buddha. Other religions include Taoism, Christianity, and Islam. Different cultures within China often have different religious beliefs.

Nearly all Chinese people aim for a sense of balance. For some, this balance is possible through the ideas of yin and yang. Yin represents a female force that is cool and calm. Yang represents a male force that is hot and active. When both of these ideals are present, balance is achieved.

◆ This symbol represents the ideas of yin and yang.

CHAPTER FOUR

CELEBRATIONS

Music and parades are important parts of many Chinese holidays.

The people of China work hard. But they know how to enjoy themselves, too. They take part in games, sports, and holidays. Many people, for example, play chess and mahjong.

Mahjong is similar to the card game rummy. But it is played with decorated tiles instead of cards. The game originated in China. Today, it is one of the country's most popular games.

Mahjong playing pieces

The national sport of China is table tennis. Other favorites include soccer, basketball, and swimming. Many Chinese people practice tai chi. This is a graceful, slow form of martial arts. They also practice other forms of martial arts, such as tae kwon do and kung fu.

In 2008, China hosted the Summer Olympic Games. That year, China won all of the individual medals for table tennis as well as gold medals in the team competitions. Chinese athletes had strong scores in gymnastics, too.

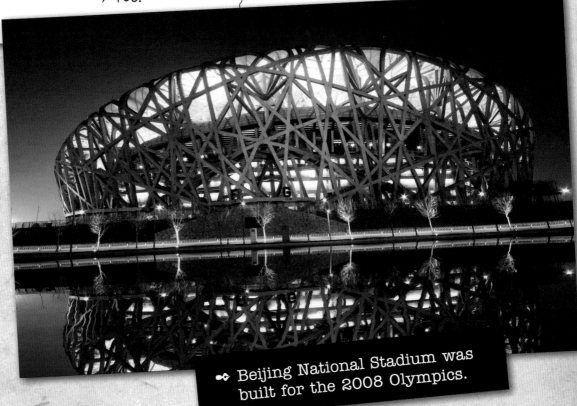

❖ Beijing National Stadium was built for the 2008 Olympics.

➥ Elaborate dragon costumes are a common sight during Chinese New Year.

In China, the biggest holiday is Chinese New Year. It is sometimes called the Spring Festival. This celebration is usually held in January or February. It lasts for 2 weeks. There are parties, parades, and fireworks. For the parades, many people dress in dragon costumes.

Would you like to decorate your room for Chinese New Year? Try making paper lanterns. These are often a part of Chinese New Year celebrations. Here's how to make one. Try making several and stringing them together. A word of caution: these lanterns are only meant for decoration. Do not place a candle, light bulb, or other heat source inside them!

MATERIALS:

- Construction paper (several colors)
- Scissors
- Tape, glue, or a stapler

INSTRUCTIONS:

1. Fold a piece of construction paper in half lengthwise. You should now have a rectangle.

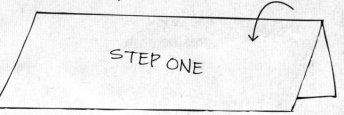

STEP ONE

2. Make at least 12 cuts along the fold. Space the cuts evenly. Make sure you don't cut all the way to the opposite edge of the paper.

STEP TWO

3. Unfold the paper. Join the shorter sides of the paper together to create a tube. Tape, glue, or staple the points where the paper meets along the top and bottom of the tube.

STEP THREE

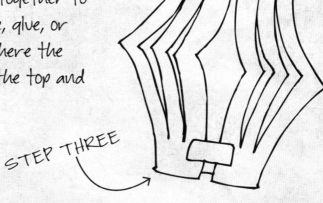

4. For a handle, cut a strip of paper. It should be 6 inches (15.2 centimeters) long and 0.5 inches (1.3 cm) wide. Bend the strip into an arch. Tape, glue, or staple the ends of the strip to the top of your lantern.

STEP FOUR

Have fun experimenting with different colors of paper.

Another important holiday is the Dragon Boat Festival. People celebrate with river parades and dragon boat races.

Dragon Boat Fesitval

These are some national holidays in China:

January–February (date varies): Chinese New Year

March 8: International Women's Day

May 1: Labor Day

June 1: International Children's Day

October 1: National Day

WHAT'S FOR DINNER?

➤ Chinese cuisine features a wide variety of unique and flavorful foods.

Have you ever been to a Chinese restaurant? Some restaurants serve traditional Chinese food. There are many different types of Chinese **cuisine**. You could spend a long time getting familiar with all of the delicious options that Chinese food has to offer.

When you think of Chinese food, what comes to mind? Rice? It is true that rice is a part of many Chinese meals. But Chinese food often features many other ingredients. These include noodles, potatoes, tofu, meat, and fish. Chinese dumplings are popular, too. They are usually filled with meat or vegetables. Some regions use very little meat. Most Chinese dishes are made without milk, cheese, or other dairy products.

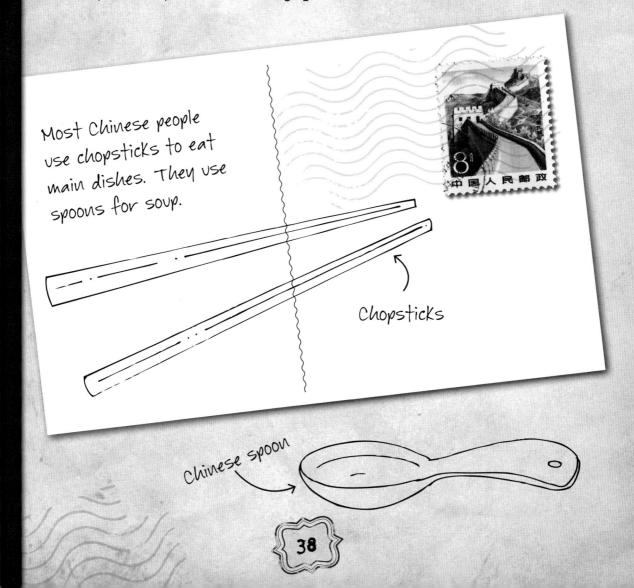

Most Chinese people use chopsticks to eat main dishes. They use spoons for soup.

Chopsticks

Chinese spoon

○ Noodles, meat, and vegetables can all be found in many Cantonese dishes.

Chinese food varies from province to province. Canton cuisine is found in Guangdong province and Hong Kong in southern China. Fresh ingredients are used. Sauces are mild. That way, the fresh flavors of food are not overpowered. Popular Cantonese dishes include roast suckling pig and crispy chicken.

→ Pot stickers are filled with different blends of meat and vegetables.

Mandarin cuisine is often found in Beijing. Meals are often very beautiful, with vegetables carved into flowers and other designs. Wheat may be used instead of rice in Mandarin dishes. One well-known Mandarin dish is pan-fried pot stickers.

Do you like hot and spicy foods? Sichuan cuisine is right for you. Many of the dishes are made with peppers. Popular dishes include cold noodles with peanut sauce and stir-fried green beans.

Hunan cuisine is even hotter. These dishes use strong oils, sauces, and garlic. Some well-known dishes are orange chicken and spicy eggplant.

Shanghai cuisine features full flavors that are the result of slow-cooked sauces. Popular dishes include pickled greens with pork.

◆ Pork is featured in many Chinese recipes.

Many Chinese people enjoy hot tea. They drink it with meals and throughout the day. Soup is often part of Chinese meals, too. Don't forget desert! Almond cookies, fruits, and puddings are some options.

➦ Cookies and fruit make great deserts no matter what country you're in!

There are many different Chinese foods you can cook with your family. Here is a recipe to start with. Ask an adult to help, especially with the steps that involve slicing or heating.

Steamed Pears with Honey

INGREDIENTS
2 Asian or Bartlett pears
4 teaspoons (19.7 milliliters) of honey
2 dried Chinese dates (you could also use other dates or raisins)

Instructions are on the following page

INSTRUCTIONS

1. Soak the dates in cold water until soft. Carefully cut them in half and remove the pits.

2. Rinse and dry the pears. Slice off the tops of the pears. Save the tops for step #7.

3. Cut out the cores to create a hollow space.

4. If needed, cut off parts of the bottom of each pear so it will sit up.

5. Spoon 2 teaspoons (9.9 ml) of honey into the hollow space of each pear.

6. Insert a date (or several raisins if you don't have dates) inside the hollow space of each pear.

7. Place the tops of the pears back on, as if they were lids.

8. You will need a steamer to cook the pears. Ask an adult to set up a bamboo steamer, steaming rack, or other steaming device according to its specific directions. Have the adult set the pears inside the steamer. Steam for 30 minutes or until the pears are tender. Have the adult carefully remove the pears.

9. Serve while the fruit is still warm.

Is mealtime important in your family? Throughout China, families often take the time to sit down and enjoy meals together.

Have your discoveries about China left you wanting more? Your investigations don't have to stop here, culture explorer. Maybe one day you'll be able to visit China and soak up the wonders of this amazing country!

➥ Chinese works of art often feature dragon designs.

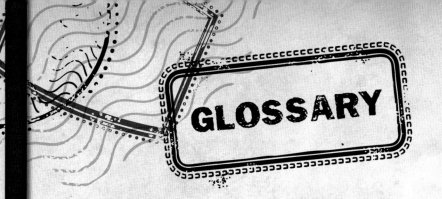

GLOSSARY

autonomous (aw-TAH-nuh-muhss) having to do with being independent or governing oneself

communist (KOM-yuh-nist) having to do with a type of government in which property belongs to the community or government

cuisine (kwi-ZEEN) a style or way of cooking or presenting food

endangered (en-DAYN-jurd) at risk of dying out completely

ethnic (ETH-nik) having to do with a group of people who have the same culture or history

export (EK-sport) a product that is sent to another country to be sold there

import (IM-port) to bring a product into a country from another country

mainland (MAYN-luhnd) the main or largest land mass of a country, rather than its islands or other areas

minority (muh-NOR-uh-tee) a group of people of a certain race or religion living among a larger group of a different race or religion

plateaus (pla-TOHZ) areas of high, flat land

provinces (PROV-uhnss-iz) areas or regions of some countries

rural (RUR-uhl) having to do with the country or farming

urban (UR-buhn) having to do with cities

FOR MORE INFORMATION

Books

Friedman, Mel. *China*. New York: Children's Press, 2008.

Hardyman, Robyn. *Celebrate China*. New York: Chelsea Clubhouse, 2009.

McCulloch, Julie. *China*. Chicago: Heinemann Library, 2009.

Web Sites

BBC—The Culture Club: The Chinese New Year
www.bbc.co.uk/northernireland/schools/4_11/cultureclub/ learning/chinainfo.shtml
Find a lot of information about an important Chinese celebration.

National Geographic Kids—China
kids.nationalgeographic.com/Places/Find/China
Learn more about China, past and present.

TIME For Kids—Native Lingo—China
www.timeforkids.com/TFK/kids/hh/goplaces/ article/0,28376,536989,00.html
Listen to sound clips of some common Mandarin Chinese phrases.

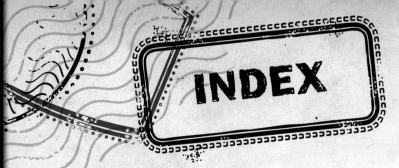

INDEX

ABOUT THE AUTHOR
Lucia Raatma has written dozens of books for young readers. Her favorite Chinese dish is spicy peanut noodles. She and her family live in the Tampa Bay area of Florida.